ISBN 0-7683-2097-6

Text by Flavia and Lisa Weedn
Illustrations by Flavia Weedn
© Weedn Family Trust
www.flavia.com
All rights reserved.

Published in 1999 by Cedco Publishing Company
100 Pelican Way, San Rafael, California 94901
For a free catalog of other Cedco® products, please write
to the address above, or visit our website: www.cedco.com

Printed in Hong Kong

1 3 5 7 9 10 8 6 4 2

The artwork for each picture is digitally mastered using acrylic on canvas.

With love and gratitude to those talented souls who made this book a reality—
Rick Weedn, Lisa Mansfield, Diana Musacchio, Jane Durand, Tyler Tomblin,
Heather Day, Solveig Chandler, Hui-Ying Ting-Bornfreund and Annette Berlin.

The human spirit is miraculous

in its capacity to heal,

for it is made of hope and strength

and the ever-present power of love.

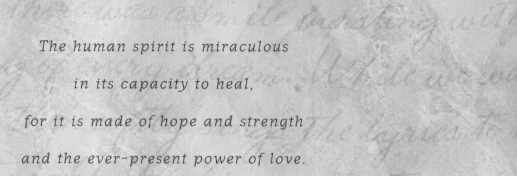

This is my story.

_____

written by

_____

date

Other Flavia Books:

To Take Away the Hurt

Flavia and Lisa Weedn
Illustrated by Flavia Weedn

Cedco Publishing Company • San Rafael, California

Heartache, like love, is a part of life's journey. It touches us all.

To feel and to love deeply is a divine gift; its miracle can light

our way through the darkest storm. Life holds hidden

treasures in its hands, and even the most painful of our

experiences can lead us to awakenings that bring us

closer to our faith and help us to become more.

When a sacred part of us feels broken and torn, we need only

look within, for inside each of us there is a place born of the

human spirit – a place of profound strength and courage.

When we are called to reach for it, we find that its truth can help us

better understand the essence of who we are, as we learn

of our own heart's endless capacity to love.

This journal is designed to be a safe place in which your

soul can rest. May it become a soothing shelter where you

rediscover cherished moments you may have thought were

lost. May you find wisdom and laughter where you least expect it,

and a radiant light of hope where you once saw only shadow.

May you find comfort as you fill these pages with your story

for amid all the joy and sadness, yours is a beautiful tale of living.

When you finally close this book, we pray you will embrace

the precious healer time can be – and find yourself

at peace, unbroken, and richly blessed for every moment

of love your life has known.

Flavia

Table of Contents

The Empty Places

Echoes of Comfort

Courageous Spirit

Soulful Awakenings

Remembering Joy • Cherished Moments

Footprints in the Sand • Lingering Touch

A Part of Me • Forever and Always

Honoring the Gift in My Heart

Finding Comfort • Recovering Truth

Lessons of Life • Legacies of Love

New Beginnings

Gazing Upon the Horizon

The Promise of Tomorrow

God's Grace • Giving Thanks

With Reverence and Respect

Blessing the Memory

Embracing the Moment

Holding Close the Beauty

Hope and Healing

Path of Prayer • Journey of Hope

Restoring Faith • Unbroken Dreams

Embracing the Dawn • Finding Clarity

Rebuilding Foundations • Believing in Me

Unexpected Miracles • Becoming More

Out of the Shadows Into the Light

I wish I could

take away the hurt

and **soothe** the

empty place inside

your **heart** where

tears are born.

The Empty Places

Defining the Hurt

Feeling the Vacancy

Silent tears hurt the most. Tell me of your hurt and my heart will listen.

The Deepest Ache

The Questioning

In Search of

Understanding

Someday,
beyond
the clouds,
there will
be love,
compassion
and justice,
and we
shall all
understand.

The Hardest Mile

Letting Go

In the Silence

Talking to God

Reaching Out

Looking Within

Listen to

the voice

of your

HEART.

It is wiser

than you know.

Echoes of Comfort

Thoughts Unspoken

Treasures Untold

Life's moments are woven into songs and silences only the heart can hear.

Private Yearnings

Leftover Dreams

Trusting the Voice

Of My Heart

Your
heart
is
your
inner
compass.
Its
truth
will
guide
you
home.

Seeking the Truth

Of My Soul

What I Believe

Echoes of Faith

To

believe

is to

know we

are never

alone,

that life

is a gift,

and this

is our

time to

cherish

it.

Mysteries Unveiled

The Beauty Within

Strength

is born of LOVE

and nothing is

impossible to the

believing heart.

Courageous Spirit

Discovering Strength

Finding Courage

The
gifts
we
receive
are not
always
those
wrapped
in ribbons,
some are
born of
the
heart.

Cleansing Tears

Facing the Fears

Soothing Surrender

Calming the Storm

We are all beacons of light. Trust in yourself and embrace the hope that lives within you.

Tides of Change

Facing the Sun

Finding Forgiveness

For Myself and Others

Compassion is a gift from God. Understanding is the song of angels.

Angels of Wisdom

Messengers of Peace

*T*hat which

brings us

SADNESS has once

brought us joy.

Cherish all

that was *yours*.

Soulful Awakenings

Remembering Joy

Cherished Moments

Some people leave footprints on our hearts, and we are never, ever the same.

Footprints in the Sand

Lingering Touch

A Part of Me

Forever and Always

If you
look
you will
find me.
I will be
translucent,
flickering
wings between
the sun
and sky.

Honoring the Gift

In My Heart

Finding Comfort

Recovering Truth

That which the heart has cherished becomes a part of us forever.

Lessons of Life

Legacies of Love

$\mathcal{T}$o believe

is to know that

every **day** is a

new **beginning**.

It is to trust that

miracles happen.

Hope and Healing

Path of Prayer

Journey of Hope

Believe with your heart that life is happening exactly as it was meant to.

Restoring Faith

Unbroken Dreams

Embracing the Dawn

Finding Clarity

Life holds hidden gifts in its hands, and gives them to each of us when it is time.

Rebuilding Foundations

Believing in Me

Unexpected Miracles

Becoming More

We

are

unaware

of what

sweet

miracles

may

come.

Out of the Shadows

Into the Light

There are

no endings

in life,

only new

beginnings.

New Beginnings

Gazing Upon

The Horizon

Time

is a friend,

a healer,

a maker

of dreams.

The Promise

Of Tomorrow

God's Grace

Giving Thanks

We

are each

a part

of one

another.

Care is

the golden

thread that

connects

us all.

With Reverence

And Respect

Blessing the Memory

Embracing the Moment

Time

and

distance

have no

meaning.

Love is the

beauty we

take with

us wherever

we go.

Holding Close

The Beauty

Flavia

Lisa and her daughter Sylvie

Photos by Chris Chandler

Flavia Weedn is one of America's leading inspirational writers and illustrators. Her work, and the work of her daughter and co-author, Lisa Weedn, celebrates life and offers hope to the human spirit.

Their collaborative work has touched the lives of millions through books, cards, posters, fine stationery products, and hundreds of licensed goods throughout the world.

Flavia and Lisa live in Santa Barbara, California.

Hope

Heart